The Poet's Voice

Sherry Weese-Anthamatten

bush PUBLISHING & associates

The Poet's Voice
ISBN: 978-0-9967285-1-5
Copyright © 2015 by Sherry Weese-Anthamatten

Bush Publishing & Associates books may be ordered at
www.bushpublishing.com or www.amazon.com.

For further information, please contact:
Bush Publishing & Associates
www.bushpublishing.com

Contents

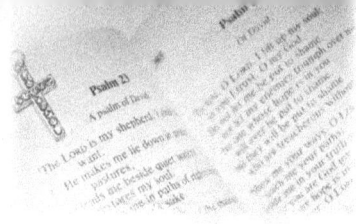

Still Water

Once I was so tired, so overwhelmed
I knew, I just couldn't go on
So, I cried out, to Jesus, "Lord, won't you help me,
I don't even know where I went wrong."

All of a sudden, the strength left my body
I fell to the ground, on my face
The presence of God, so heavy upon me
I just had to rest, in His grace

Just like a dead man, with no strength to stand
I lay, on my face, at His feet
Then, deep on the inside, I heard this word
In a voice, indescribably sweet

He said, "I'll give you rest and make you lie down
In pastures, so cool and green
And, as my still water, flows through your spirit
It washes and makes you clean."

Come and drink deeply, from the pool of still water
The power of healing, will make you whole
The peace that surpasses your understanding
Is in the still water that restores your soul

Sherry L. Anthamatten © 1997
Poetry, Prayer and Praise Vol. I.

The Lord is my shepherd, I shall not want
He maketh me to lie down in green pastures,
He leadeth me beside the still waters
He restoreth my soul.

Psalms 23:1-3

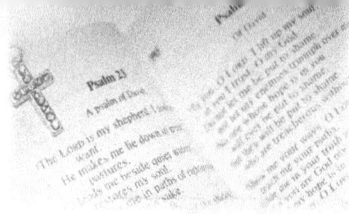

Peace and Balance

A delicate scale of balance: Moderation in all things
A quiet place that gives me strength, for life and all it brings
The narrow path lies well within, the boundaries of extremes
Upon that firm foundation, I will walk in perfect peace

Like a hillside in the country, where thought and vision clear
As I behold the face of God, He whispers in my ear
"A method to the madness; a purpose to the plan"
The place to lay my burden down, is in the Master's hand

Sherry L. Anthamatten© 1998
Poetry, Prayer and Praise Vol. II.

Thou will keep him in perfect peace
whose mind is stayed on thee

Isaiah 26:3

Be well-balanced (temperate, sober of a mind)

Isaiah 30:15 (Amplified Bible)

Come unto me, all ye that labor and are heavy laden,
and I will give you rest.

Matthew 11:28

Whispers From Heaven

Tonight I come to lay my broken life down at your feet
All others have forsaken me, but you are all I need
Voices spin around me 'til I think I'll lose my mind
But you will be my hiding place, and perfect peace I'll find
For you alone, can see my heart and know my suffering
For me, you suffered more than I could know
But I can make it through this night
and everything will be alright
If I can hear you whisper to me
Whisper to me Jesus.
No other voice could ever sound as sweet
Whisper to me Jesus.
Your word is like a lamp unto my feet

Sherry L. Anthamatten © 2001
Poetry, Prayer and Praise Vol. IV.

Today if ye will hear His voice,
harden not your hearts…

Hebrews 3:15

And thine ears shall hear a word behind thee saying,
"This is the way, walk ye in it."

Isaiah 30:21

Thy word is a lamp unto my feet,
and a light unto my path.

Psalms 119:105

Not Forgotten

I have not forgotten you, know that I care
And hear with compassion, each word of your prayer
Whereever you're going, whatever you do
Remember, my eye is always, on you

I haven't forgotten one word, of your prayer
The shout of your victory, your moan of despair
My child, if you listen, you will surely hear me
As you whisper, "Amen", saying, "Yes, let it be"

Sherry L. Anthamatten © 1998
Poetry, Prayer and Praise Vol. II.

For all the promises of God in Him
are Yea and in Him, Amen

II. Corinthians 1:20

He forgetteth not the cry of the humble

Psalms 9:12

For the eyes of the Lord are on the righteous
and His ears are attentive to their prayer

I. Peter 3:12
(New International Version)

For God is not unrighteous to forget
your work and labor of love, which
ye have shewed toward his name

Hebrews 6:10

A Word to Describe Him

If I could write a brand-new word
That's never been spoken and never been heard
A word to describe a God who's so good
He gives undeserved favor to me

A God so full of mercy and love
Yet all power on Earth and in Heaven, above
He holds in the palm of His mighty hand
And He offers to share it with me

He is the King of the universe. There's no one else like Him
He is Alpha and Omega, the Beginning and the End
Yet the greatest desire of His heart is for me
Just to love Him and know Him as Friend

If I could write a brand new word
That has never been spoken and never been heard
I'd describe a great God who came down from His throne
To a world lost and dying, without light or hope

A Shepherd who's willing to leave His whole flock
To seek and to rescue one lamb that is lost
I ask, "What shall I call one who made such a plan?"
His answer is simply, "I Am That I Am"!

… *For I am God, and there is none else; I am God,*
and there is none like me.

Isaiah 46:9

Thus saith of the Lord thy Redeemer and
He that formed thee from the womb,
I am the Lord that maketh all things;
that stretches forth the heavens alone;
that spreadeth abroad the earth by myself

Isaiah 44:24

… *They shall say to me, What is his name?*
What shall I say unto them?
And God said unto Moses, "I AM THAT I AM."

Exodus 3:13–14

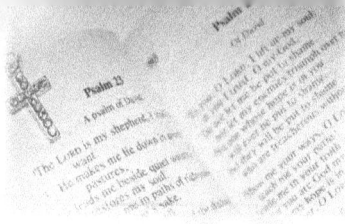

In a Moment

Lord and God of all creation
First and true love of my heart
One day soon now, I will know of you
What I have only known in part

I will watch for you each day and night
'Til the moment you appear
With the words, I've longed and waited for
Calling, "Children, come up here!"

We will rise together, like the clouds
Past the bonds of earth and space
As we rush into your open arms
Where we will see you face to face

Lord and God of all creation
First and true love of my heart
In that moment I will know of you
What I have only known in part

Sherry L. Anthamatten© 1998
Poetry, Prayer and Praise Vol. II.

And they heard a great voice from heaven
saying unto them, "Come up here."
And they ascended up to heaven in a cloud.

Revelation 11:12

In a moment, in the twinkling of an eye,
at the last trump:

I Corinthians 15:52

Now I know in part; but then I shall know even
as I am known. For now we see through
a glass darkly; but then face to face.

I Corinthians 13:12

Walking With Jesus

I'm walking in the grace, of my Lord, Jesus
I've got His angels watching over me
I don't have to carry those heavy burdens
I cast my cares on Him, and He cares for me

I don't have to worry, what I will say
When I stand before the judges of this world
I will follow, as His Spirit leads me
The words of His wisdom, are my pearls

I'm walking with Jesus, and life is sweet
He works all things together for my good
He laid His life down, just to save me
And all my debts were paid, with Holy blood

I walk by faith and not by sight
It's by His Spirit, not by might
I've got His angels watching over me
I don't have to be afraid,
I know His mercy's new each day
I cast my cares on him, and He cares for me

Sherry L. Anthamatten© 1997
Poetry, Prayer and Praise Vol. I.

For we walk by faith, not by sight:

II Corinthians 5:7

Not by might, nor by power, but by my Spirit,
Saith the Lord of hosts.

Zachariah 4:6

Casting all your care upon Him; for He careth for you.

I Peter 5:6–7

The Body of Christ

I love being part, of this family
We're all brothers and sisters, in Christ
When I look into the faces, around me
I see the love of our Lord, in your eyes

As we gather together, of one accord
To worship and honor and glorify the Lord
His love is shed abroad, in the hearts of His own
And through us, His love is made known

Jesus has made us, all fishers of men
So we cast out our nets, to bring His people in
As His gift of saving grace, to each heart is revealed
By His Spirit, our nets will be filled

Sherry Lynn Anthamatten © 1997
Poetry, Prayer and Praise Vol. I.

So we being many, are one body in Christ,
and every one members one of another.

Romans 12:5

There is neither Jew nor Greek,
there is neither bond nor free,
there is neither male nor female:
for ye are all one in Christ Jesus.

Galatians 3:28

Don't Let Go

Don't give up when you get down
The Lord's going to turn this thing around
Don't let go 'til you get the victory!

The word of God will come alive
And when it opens up your eyes
You'll know the truth, and it will set you free!

Just hold on with all your might
Everything's going to be alright
Trust in Him to meet your every need!

Don't let go 'til you get the victory!

Just keep on and don't look back
The Word of God will light your path
And will be a lamp unto your feet!

The world can never satisfy
The emptiness you feel inside
But, Jesus Christ can make your life complete!

No matter what you're going through
There's nothing that the Lord can't do
Anything you'll ask and believe!

Don't let go 'til you get the victory!

But thanks be to God, which giveth us the victory
through our Lord Jesus Christ.
Therefore, my beloved brethren, be steadfast,
unmovable always abounding in the work of the Lord,
for as much as ye know that your labor is
not in vain in the Lord.

I Corinthians 15:57–58

A Miracle For You

I asked the Lord, Jesus, "Lord, what can I give?"
He answered, "My child, just give what you have."
It seemed so little, but all that I had
Were two little fishes and a few loaves of bread
So, I laid my basket down, at His feet
Thanking the Lord, for all He'd given me
He accepted my offering, to be used as seed
Asked the Father to bless it and bring the increase
Then, I watched the miracle, Jesus would do
From my little basket, He fed the multitude!

So, bring your gifts to Jesus, no matter how small
And offer them to Him, with thanks, in your heart
You'll see what the blessing, of Jesus, can do
The Lord has a miracle, for you!

I was lost in the desert, with no place to hide
An army, of enemy, closing in behind
Up ahead, a great ocean stood in the way
Of my only hope, of escape
So, there in the desert, I fell on my knees
And cried out, "Oh God, It's a miracle I need!"
He said, "Lift up your staff and speak to the sea."
Then, He parted the waters for me!

So, when you're in trouble and see no way out
Let the Word of God rise up, in your mouth
Then, stand on the Promise and see what He'll do
The Lord has a miracle, for you!

⚮

*There is a lad here, which hath five barley loaves,
and two small fishes: but what are they
among so many?*

John 6:9

*Give from what you have.
If you want to give, your gift will be accepted.
It will be judged by what you have,
not by what you do not have.*

*II. Corinthians 8:12
(New Century Version)*

*But the salvation of the righteous is of the Lord:
He is their strength in times of trouble.
And the Lord shall help them, and deliver them:
He shall deliver them from the wicked, and save
them, because they trust in him.*

Psalms 37:39–40

Face to Face

Lord, you are the Rose of Sharon, you're the Bright and
Morning Star
Altogether Lovely, that's who you are
Eye has never seen, throughout earth or space
Anything to compare Lord, with your glorious face
Look down on me Jesus, fill me with your grace
And draw me by your Spirit, 'til we're standing face to face

When Moses came down from the mount, his face
shone like the sun
What glorious things he must have seen, in your
presence there, oh God
You say you'll give me what I ask, so my deepest heart's
desire
Is to see you in your glory, and to feel your holy fire
Jesus, thank you for your goodness, for your mercy's
new each day
But if I could ask just one more thing, I want to see you
face to face

Sherry Lynn Anthamatten © 1997
Poetry, Prayer and Praise Vol. I.

When thou saidst, "Seek ye my face;
my heart said unto thee, Thy face, Lord, I will seek."

Psalms 27:8

"His servants shall worship Him;
they shall see Him face to face."

Revelation 22:4
(New English Bible)

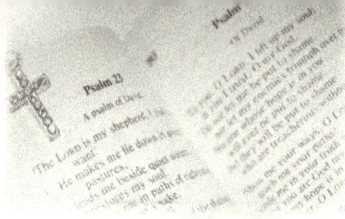

Fan The Flame

Open up your eyes and look around you
Your brothers and your sisters are in need
The fire of the Lord that once burned in their hearts
Is flickering like a flame that's growing weak

You can help a friend and bring about a change
He says, "where two or more of you are gathered in my name"
Just one touch from Jesus and we'll never be the same
So, stand upon His Word and fan the flame

The Lord commands us all to love each other
And that our brother's burden we should bear
When the devil comes to kill, to steal and to destroy
We have to lift our brother up in prayer

Holy Spirit, fall upon your people
Jesus, we call upon your name
Send your Holy Spirit, like a mighty rushing wind
To blow through this house and fan the flame

Sherry L. Anthamatten © 1997
Poetry, Prayer and Praise Vol. I.

… Stir up (rekindle the embers of,
fan the flame of and keep burning)
the (gracious) gift of God,
(the inner fire) that is in you…

II.Timothy 1:6
(Amplified Bible)

A bruised reed He will not break,
and a dimly burning wick He will not quench.

Isaiah 42:3
(Amplified Bible)

Bear ye one another's burdens,
and so fulfill the law of Christ.

Galatians 6:2

Father's Family

You've been out there for so long
Trying to make it on your own
Hanging on, just trying not to give in
But, you know there's something wrong
It's like you just don't belong
To this world, you try so hard to fit in

That's why I had to come and find you
If you will only hear what I say
This world is not the home, you belong to
That's the reason why you're feeling this way

You're of the Father's family
And if you'll follow me
I will lead you back unto your Father
You were always meant to be
In the Father's family
Where you are born again, to live forever!

He's the shepherd of His flock
And if even one gets lost
The Father never rests until He finds you
That's why He sent His Son
To that lost and lonely one
So that safely, back home, He could guide you

If you will look to Him and no other
You'll never have to go it alone
Just come and meet your sisters and your brothers
They're going to be so glad to have you home!

You're of the Father's family
When we get there, you will see
He has a "homecoming party" waiting for you!
All the angels will rejoice
As you hear the Father's voice
Say, "Welcome home, my child, I've waited for you!"

*For the Son of man is come to seek
and to save that which was lost.*

Luke 19:10

God sets the lonely in families:

*Psalm 68:6
(New International Version)*

*Now you are no longer strangers to God
and foreigners to heaven,
but you are members of God's very own family,
citizens of God's country,
and you belong in God's household
with every other Christian.*

*Ephesians 3:19 T
(The Living Bible)*

Feed My Lambs

Jesus says to us, "Feed my lambs"
Sometimes they need a helping hand
If they're hungry, will you feed them?
If they're wandering, will you lead them?
"Feed my lambs" then, lead them home, again

Jesus says to us, "Love one another"
Please don't turn away from your brother
If he's hungry, will you feed him?
If he's lost his way, will you lead him?
"Feed my lambs" then, lead them home, again

The Lord says, "as you've done to the least of these
That you've also done to the King of Kings"
If you freely give, as He freely gave
You can lead someone to the Lord, today
He's the Lamb! That takes away our sin
And by His loving hand, He leads us home, again

Sherry L. Anthamatten © 1997
Poetry Prayer and Praise Vol. I.

Jesus saith to Simon Peter, "Simon, son of Jonas,
lovest thou me more than these?
… Feed my lambs

John 21:15

For the Lamb which is in the midst of the throne
shall feed them, and shall lead them into
living fountains of waters:

Revelation 7:17

Prayer of Intercession

Someone is hurting, Lord, wounded and weak
But Father, you know our need
So I will come boldly, before your throne
Oh God, let my prayer intercede

Let your Spirit come on him with power and peace
Giving strength to stand on his own
Let me stand in the gap for my brother, oh God
As I bow at the foot of your throne

The prayer of the righteous, availeth so much
And I am made righteous in Him
The life that I live is no longer my own
It's not I, but Jesus who lives

Let us love each other, as you loved us all
And lift up our brother, that he might not fall
We pray, your Spirit, to fill us with power
To stand, in this final hour

Sherry L. Anthamatten © 1997
Poetry, Prayer and Praise Vol. I..

Pray one for another that ye may be healed.
The effectual fervent prayer of a righteous man
availeth much

James 5:16

I am crucified with Christ: nevertheless I live;
yet not I, but Christ liveth in me

Galatians 2:20

Let us therefore come boldly unto the throne of grace
That we may obtain mercy and find grace
to help in time of need.

Hebrews 4:16

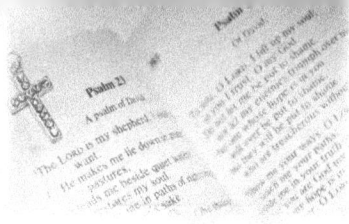

Love Of My Life

The Lord says my Spirit comes to testify of me
He will reveal to you life's greatest mystery
How God so loved the world, He gave His only Son
And I gave my life for you, washed you in my own blood

You're the love of my life. You're the love of my life
I won't settle for part, I want all of your heart
You're the love of my life, You're the love of my life
Your new life can start, let me into your heart.

I was your lost child, but Lord, You remembered me
I was the lonely one 'til you came and walked with me
I'd be the last one to ever be worthy
Of the great gift of love, Father, you gave to me

You're the love of my life. You're the love of my life
Lord, I need a new start, please come into my heart
You're the love of my life. You're the love of my life
I won't offer you part, I give you all of my heart

You are my first love, Lord, I return to thee
You are the only love that I will ever need
You are my last love and through eternity
It will be your love that lives inside of me

You're the love of my life. You're the love of my life
I won't offer you part, I give you all of my heart
You're the love of my life. You're the love of my life
If I don't give it all, I'm giving nothing at all

❦❧

Greater love hath no man than this,
that a man lay down His life for His friend

John 15:13

A Mother's Heart

Sometimes I wonder, Mary, virgin blessed of God
How you must have felt, holding the Savior in your arms
Could a mother's heart so full of love, hope to understand
That the babe you now hold to your breast, would save
the world from sin

How merciful, Our Father; how wonderful His plan
To come, born of a woman, Son of God and Son of Man

In the beginning was The Word, and The Word was God
Made flesh, He dwelt among us, but the world received
Him not
They shouted crucify Him, but even on that day
He prayed, "Father forgive them", as all our debts He paid

How merciful, Our Father; how wonderful His plan
Saved by the blood of Jesus, Son of God and Son of Man

Sometimes I wonder, Mary, woman blessed of God
How you must have felt, holding the Savior in your arms
Could a mother's heart so full of love, give you strength
to stand
From the hour they laid Him in the tomb, 'til the day He
rose again

How merciful, Our Father; how wonderful His plan
Jesus reigns forever, Son of God and Son of Man

Sherry L. Anthamatten © 1997
Poetry, Prayer and Praise Vol. 1.

*...and the virgin's name was Mary.
And the angel came in unto her,
And said, Hail, thou that art highly favoured,
the Lord is with thee:
Blessed art thou among women.*

Luke 1:28

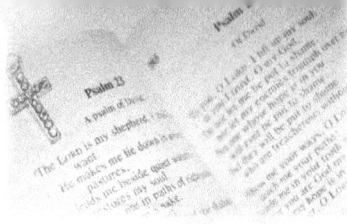

Prayer Of Faith

You might be praying, "Father, do you hear me?"
'Cause the answer you need, hasn't come
Have faith in my promise, and trust in my plan
And don't you ever give up!

I hear what you're praying for, I know what you need
But, you have to be willing to wait
And though I don't answer, a minute too soon
I'll never be one minute late

I can do anything, and I will do everything
If you will just trust and believe
That I can do anything, and I will do everything
When you put your faith in me!

Sometimes when I pray, I ask, "Lord do you hear me?"
'Cause the answer I need, hasn't come
But, I stand on your promise, I trust in your plan
And I won't ever give up!

You hear what I'm praying for. You know what I need
But, I have to be willing to wait
And though you don't answer, a minute too soon
I know you won't be too late!

'Cause, you can do anything, and you will do everything
If I will just trust and believe
That you can do anything, and you will do everything
Because of your love for me

Sherry L. Anthamatten © 1997
Poetry, Prayer and Praise Vol. I.

And Jesus answering saith unto them, Have faith in God. For verily I say unto you, That whosoever shall say unto this mountain, Be thou removed, and be thou cast into the sea; and shall not doubt in his heart, but shall believe that those things which he saith shall come to pass; he shall have whatsoever he saith. Therefore I say unto you, What things soever ye desire, when ye pray, believe that ye receive them, and ye shall have them.

Mark 11:22-24

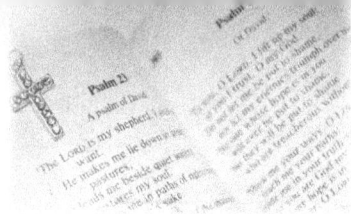

Second Chances

You might think that your life has already gone too far
Nobody knows the heartache that's made you what you are
You might think it's too late to turn the clock back, now

I know where you're coming from 'cause I've been
there, my friend
But, Jesus will forgive you, no matter where you've been
He'll put your past behind you, and you can start again

He's the God of Second Chances; He can turn it all
around
He knows all about you and loves you anyhow
He's the God of Second Chances, give God a chance
right now!

If you've really had enough but, don't know what to do
If you just feel like giving up, Jesus is good news!
He's got all the answers; what have you got to lose?

He's the God of Second Chances, when you need a
brand new start
He knows all about the heartache, that's tearing you apart
He's the God of Second Chances, just let Him have your
heart!

...for the Lord your God is gracious and merciful
and will not turn away His face from you,
if ye return to Him

II. Chronicles 30:9

Therefore if any man be in Christ,
He is a new creature: old things have passed away;
behold, all things are become new.

II. Corinthians 5:17

A Crown

Oh, Father, hear my prayer
And grant me a crown to wear
So, as I stand before your throne
I might have a crown of gold
And when the face of my Savior I see
That I might cast my crown at His feet

There is no other reason, I know
I'd have a need of a crown of gold
But to lay at the nail-scarred feet
Of the Lamb who was slain for me

As the angels of God, encircle His throne
Crying, "Holy is the Lamb that was slain"
All the saints will worship Him, casting down crowns
And one by one, He will call us by name

Oh, Father, hear my prayer
And grant me a crown to wear
So, as I stand before your throne
I might have a crown of gold
And to lay it down at the feet
Of the Savior who died for me

"The Father has heard your prayer
And will give you a crown to wear
Guard your heart in all that you do

Let no one take your crown from you
And as you lay it down at my feet
You'll be seated in heavenly places with me"

As the angles of God, encircle His throne
Crying, "Holy is the Lamb that was slain"
All the saints will worship Him casting down crowns
And one by one, He will call us by name

Sherry Lynn Anthamatten © 1997
Poetry, Prayer and Praise Vol. I.

Henceforth there is laid up for me
a crown of righteousness,
Which the Lord, the righteous judge,
Shall give me at that day; and not to me only,
But unto all them also that love His appearing.

II. Timothy 4:8

Behold, I come quickly; hold fast which thou hast,
That no man take thy crown.

Revelation 3:11

...for I have redeemed thee,
I have called thee by thou name;
Thou art mine.

Isaiah 43:1

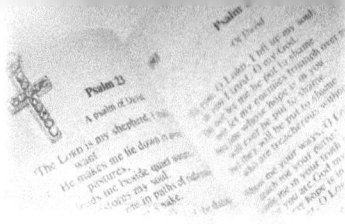

Beloved

You are the beloved, blessed of the Lord
For such a time, as this last hour,
He chose to send you forth
A vessel of His glory, to shine into the world
With purity and holiness, the Father's precious jewel
A vessel of pure gold, that has been tried with holy fire
Will carry out the mystery, of God's own heart's desire

Sherry L. Anthamatten © 1998

Poetry, Prayer and Praise Vol. II.

...thou art come to the kingdom
for such a time as this.

Esther 4:14

Blessed Hope

What joy, what joy rises up in our souls
At the sound of your name, sweet Jesus
What peace, that peace that we can't understand
The peace that knowing you brings us

What assurance and comfort is our blessed hope
That you've gone to prepare us a place
You will call out your own; we'll know as we're known
When we stand with you Lord, face to face

❧

*And the peace of God, which passeth all
understanding, shall keep your hearts
and minds through Christ Jesus.*

Philippians 4:7

*Looking for that blessed hope,
and the glorious appearing of the great God
and our Savior Jesus Christ:*

Titus 2:13

*For now we see through a glass darkly:
but then face to face: now I know in part;
but then shall I know even as also I am known*

I. Corinthians 13:12

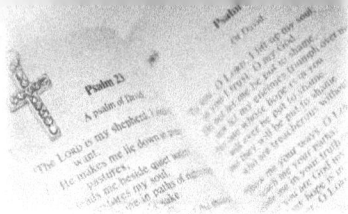

Blessing

Jehovah Jireh, my God who provides
Your goodness and faithfulness, tested and tried
The windows of heaven are poured out upon us
Who trust in our Lord, to give life in abundance
Father, we thank you for health and prosperity
For blessing your children, to make us a blessing

Sherry L. Anthamatten © 1998
Poetry, Prayer and Praise Vol. II.

And I will make of thee a great nation,
and I will bless thee,
And make thy name great;
and thou shalt be a blessing:

Genesis 12:2

Bring ye all the tithes into the storehouse,
That there may be meat in mine house,
And prove me now herewith, saith the Lord of hosts,
If I will not open you the windows of heaven,
And pour you out a blessing,
And there shall not be room enough to receive it.

Malachi 3:10

It's All About Love

From the stable, I hear a soft cry, as a baby
Is born in a most humble way
And a star in the east, is casting her light
On the manger, where Jesus is laid
A tender, young girl looks down on the child
With the comforting smile, of a mother
And somewhere above, looking down on Him, too
Are the eyes of His heavenly Father
In the still of the night, I prayed of my God
"For what purpose, have you sent your Son?"
And as songs of rejoicing, resounded through Heaven
He answered, "It's all about love!"

When Jesus had grown, and the fullness of time
Had come for divine destiny
He went into the world, calling out His disciples
Entreating them, "Come, follow me"
He spoke of His Father, and not of Himself
But often, was misunderstood
Yet all who believed, were forgiven and healed
As the Lord went about, doing good
The blind received sight, the lepers were cleansed
The dead were raised up, from the grave
He said, "I Am the Way, the Truth, and the Life
I come not to condemn, but to save!"

But, a spirit of greed, would plot against Jesus
Through one breaking bread, at His table
And deliver Him up, to the hands of accusers
With a cold-hearted kiss of betrayal
As the hour drew near, to accomplish the purpose
For which God had sent His own Son
I heard the Lord whisper this prayer, saying,
"Father not my will, but Your will, be done"

My heart gripped with terror, yet helpless, I followed
As He struggled to carry His cross
And though, all I had was my faith in His Word
It seemed, all I had would be lost

I stood frozen in place, in stark disbelief
At the sound of iron spikes, being driven
And as God's Holy Lamb poured out His own blood
For all men; He prayed, "Father, forgive them"
As He said, "It is finished!" , all the powers were shaken
On earth and in Heaven, above
As the sky turned black, I heard terrified voices cry
"Surely, He was, Son of God!"
Those who had loved Him, prepared Him for burial
And as He was laid in the grave
The Spirit of Jesus, descended to Hell
That the lost might believe, and be saved

Now, on the third day, by the power of God
In His glory, Christ Jesus is risen!
And all who believe, shall never taste death

But inherit the Life, He has given!
Again Jesus went out, unto His disciples
Saying, "Soon I must go to my Father
But, you won't be left without comfort and help
For behold, I will send you another"
"With My Spirit inside you, directing your steps
You will take My Good News to all people
That they might be saved, and redeemed from the curse
And inherit My Kingdom, eternal!"

I remember the cry of the babe, in the manger
And the sounds of rejoicing, above
My prayer, of God's purpose for sending His Son
And His answer, "It's all about love!"

*For God so loved the world,
that He gave His only begotten Son,
that whosoever believeth in Him should not perish,
but have everlasting life.*

John 3:16

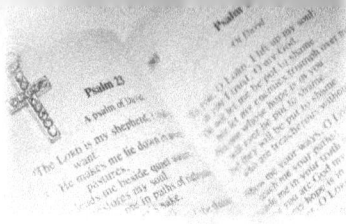

The Day of the Dancing

Listen my sisters, and you will hear
The music of heaven, is filling the air
To stir up the faith of our spirits to sing
"Let the Day of the Dancing begin!"

Let all who will worship, in spirit and truth
Come follow me now, into the throne room
Where we have been called to worship the King
"Let the Day of the Dancing begin!"

For we are the virgins, with lamps full of oil
Who long have awaited, outside heaven's door
The voice of the Bridegroom, soon now to call
"Let the Day of the Dancing begin!"

Oh worship King Jesus, and cast down your crowns
As angels sing, "Glory to God's Holy Lamb!"
Sing with the timbrels, and lift holy hands
"Let the Day of the Dancing begin!"

Sherry L. Anthamatten © 1998
Poetry, Prayer and Praise Vol. II.

But the hour cometh, and now is,
when the true worshippers
Shall worship the Father in spirit and in truth:
For the Father seeketh such to worship him.

John 4:23

Praise him with the timbrel and dance;
Let every thing that hath breath praise the Lord.

Psalms 150:4&6

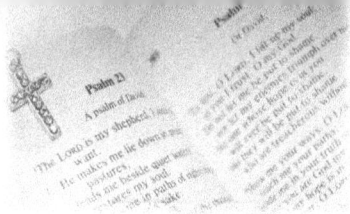

The Eyes of the Spirit

God's begun a good work, but He's not finished yet
Let's look not to what is, but to what lies ahead
Not judging each other for foolish things we might do
But let the Spirit of God, of mercy and love
Be the eyes we see through

We should look on the heart, as Jesus would do
While day by day, we're transformed and renewed
God looks on His children, whom the Son has
redeemed
From the curse of their sin, now as righteous and clean

His eyes of compassion, look past where we are
To where we are going to be
When conformed to the image and likeness of Christ
Which is truly, each child's destiny

Our God is not only the author of faith
But He is the finisher too
And He is the life that will bring forth the fruit
From the seed He has planted, in you

So let's see one another through the eyes of our Lord
Who considers each one, worth the cross that He bore
As He loved and forgave us, we must forgive too
Let the Spirit of God, of mercy and love
Be the eyes we see through

...for the Lord seeth not as man seeth;
for man looketh on the outward appearance,
But the Lord looketh on the heart.

I. Samuel 16:7

Be ye therefore merciful,
as your Father also is merciful.
Judge not, and ye shall not be judged;
condemn not, and ye shall not be condemned;
Forgive, and ye shall be forgiven.

Luke 6:36-37

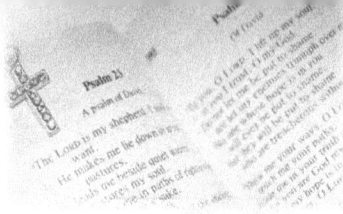

Father's Promise

My precious child, I love you; I hold you in my arms
Beneath the shadow of my wings, I shelter you from harm
Let not your heart be troubled, neither let it be afraid
You are the apple of my eye, and you are wonderfully made

Created in my image, I've predestined you to be
Conformed into my likeness, so put your trust in me
For I, the Lord alone, am God: like me, there is no other
Whatever I declare shall stand; I will do all my pleasure

The work I have begun in you, I'm faithful to complete
So lean on me, your Tower of Strength, and let your rest
be sweet
I only ask that you believe, and keep your vow to love me
And all you need, I will supply, by the riches of my glory

You see, my child, you're no mistake; I've planned you
from the start
Now hear your Father's promise: I love you with all of
my heart

Behold what manner of love the Father
hath bestowed upon us,
That we should be called the sons of God;

I John 3:1

are given unto us exceeding great promises;
That by these ye might be partakers of the divine
nature.

II Peter 1:4

Then shall the King say unto them on his right hand,
Come ye blessed of my father,
inherit the kingdom prepared for you
From the foundation of the world:

Matthew 25:34

First Fruits

Lord I give you this day, the first fruit of my week
In spirit and truth, it is you that I see
All the cares of my life, I now lay aside
Along with my thoughts, my own will and my pride
Jesus my Savior, forgiver her of sin
I confess you as Lord, and I ask once again
Be merciful to me, a sinner, oh God
Forgive me and cleanse me, with your precious blood
As I enter your rest now, I open my heart
To be still in your presence, and know you are God

For if the first fruits be holy, the lump is also holy:
And if the root be holy, so are the branches.
Romans 11:16

...the true worshippers shall worship the Father
in spirit and in truth:
For the Father seeketh such to worship Him.
John 4:23

There remaineth therefore a rest to the people of God.
For he that is entered to His rest,
He also hath ceased from his own works...
Hebrews 4:9-10

Be still and know that I am God.
Psalm 46:10

In the Flow

There is peace in the river, so stay in the flow
There is rest for the weary, in the middle of the road
Don't look to the left, or turn to the right
Make Jesus your focus; keep Him in your sight

You can walk through the flames, without feeling the heat
With God's Holy Spirit, directing your feet
You can walk on the water; He says, "Have no fear!"
"You see it is I, the Lord, drawing near"

"I give you my peace; it is all you will need"
"Don't struggle against me, but learn to receive"
"By faith, you can trust me; it's safe to let go"
"Lay down your own ways, and let me have control"

*Let thine eyes look right on,
And let thine eyelids look straight before thee.
Ponder the path of thy feet,
and let all thy ways be established.
Turn not to the right hand nor to the left*

Proverbs 4:25-27

*Trust in the Lord with all thine heart;
And lean not unto thine own understanding.
In all thy ways acknowledge Him,
and He shall direct thy paths.*

Proverbs 3:5-6

Heaven is on Its Feet

My Father, I thank you and give you the praise
For strength and endurance to finish the race
For the vision you've given and called me to do
For the cry of my heart is in following yoi

With wings of an eagle, I'll run and not faint
For the oil of your Spirit anointest you saint
With vision to see the end form beginning
Unfolding divine revelation within me

Holy Spirit of God, let me see though your eyes
As down this last stretch, I press on toward the prize
With the clock ticking faster, now loud in my ear
You have raised up your voice; your direction is clear

Up ahead I can see now, the finish draws near
And what are the sounds in the distance, I hear
A sound as if heaven is now on it's feet
With a great cloud of witnesses cheering for me!

...forgetting those things which are behind,
and reaching forth unto those things which are before,
I press toward the mark for the prize of the
high calling of God in Christ Jesus.

Philippians 3:13-14

Seeing we also are compassed about
with so great a cloud of witnesses,
Let us lay aside every weight and
the sin that doth so easily beset us
And let us run with patience {endurance}
the race that is set before us.

Hebrew 12:1

I Love You, Mighty God

I love you, beyond the confines, of this prison
Of flesh, in which now, I am bound
But my spirit is free to ascend to your heights
To rejoice in the love I have found

The prince of this world cannot steal away
The vision I've seen of your face
For this precious gift is kept out of his reach
Hidden deep, within my secret place

And he cannot enter the throne room of God
Where now, and through eternity
All of the treasures and gifts I most love
My Father has laid up for me

Oh Jesus my Savior, my Lord and my God
I lift up the voice of my praise
To the one Mighty God, I will worship and serve
And will love to the end of my days!

But thou, when thou prayest, enter into thy closet,
And when thou hast shut thy door,
Pray to thy Father which is in secret;

Matthew 6:6

Lay not up for yourselves treasures upon earth,
where moth and rust doth corrupt,
and where thieves break through and steal:
But lay up for yourselves treasures in heaven,
where neither moth nor
rust doth corrupt, and where thieves do not
break through nor steal:
For where your treasure is,
there will your heart be also.

Matthew 6:19-21

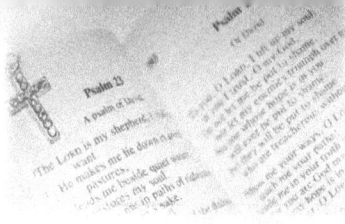

In the Name of Jesus

In the name of Jesus is the hope of my salvation
Cry my heart, "Hosanna! Jesus saves!"
In the name of Jesus, God's greatest gift is given
Mercy and compassion, by His grace

In the name of Jesus and covered by His blood
Boldly I can stand before the throne
Knowing God will hear my prayer and answer my requests
As in that Holy Name, I make them known

God's greatness is unsearchable; His ways are far above
For now, I only understand in part
But He has sent His only Son that I might know His love
And in the name of Jesus, touch His heart

Neither is there salvation in any other:
for there is none other name
under heaven given among men,
whereby we must be saved.

Acts 4:12

And whatsoever ye shall ask in my name,
that will I do, that the Father
may be glorified in the Son

John 14:13

For now we see through a glass darkly;
But then face to face;
Now I know in part; but then shall I know
even as also I am known.

1. Corinthians 13:12

Jesus Is Praying For Me

The Holy Spirit is with me, when I walk through the
desert
When I'm thirsting and dry as the sand
And He speaks to my soul, "God is still on His throne!"
"And Jesus is at His right hand!"
The Savior is there to make intercession
For those who will trust and believe
So I'm never alone and it's so good to know
That Jesus is praying for me!

The Spirit is strong but the flesh is so weak
And our enemy comes to deceive us
But his power is broken as God's Word is spoken
The Lord says He never will leave us
I am armed with the sword of God's written Word
And the joy of the Lord is my strength
Never looking behind, I press on to the prize
Thanking Jesus for praying for me!

I am only a sinner who's saved by the grace
Of the Lamb who was slain for my sins
But He stands in the gap between me and the Father
That through Him, I might enter in
To the throne room of God where the righteous are
judged

As our Lord declares, "These are redeemed!"
"So Father receive them because of my blood!"
Oh, Jesus is praying for me!

It is Christ that died, yea rather, that is risen again,
who is even at the right hand of God,
who also maketh intercession for us.

Romans 8:34

These word spake Jesus,
and lifted up his eyes to heaven
I pray for them; I pray not for the world,
But for them which thou hast given me;
for they are thine.
Neither pray I for these alone,
But for them also which shall believe on me
through their word;

John 17: 1, 9 & 20

The Light Of Your Glory

I see people, all around me. Everyone is in a hurry
They all rush and race to get somewhere
I look into their eyes and wonder if they realize
There is a God who truly cares

I see the empty stares; they seem so unaware
You gave your life so they could live
Jesus, if they only knew, that no one loves them like you do
And Father, you are faithful to forgive

Let the light of your glory shine through me
Let it be the face of Jesus they see
Let them feel your touch as I reach out, my hand
As I exalt you, Lord, Your Spirit draws all men

Holy Spirit, raise your still, small voice, I pray
And call the Father's children, in
From the darkest places, where they wonder aimlessly
Through the wilderness, of sin

I see the empty stares; they seem so unaware
You gave your life so they could live
Jesus, if they only knew that no one loves them, like
you do
And Father, you are faithful to forgive

Let the light of your glory shine through me
Let me speak the truth that sets your children free
Let it be the love of Jesus, they see
As the light of your glory shines through me.

❧

*I, the Lord, have called thee in righteousness and will
hold thine hand and will keep thee, and give thee for
a covenant of the people; for a light of the Gentiles; to
open the blind eyes, to bring out the prisoners from
the prison and them that sit in darkness
out of the prison house*

Isaiah 42:6-7

*Arise shine; for thy light is come, and the glory of the
Lord is risen upon thee. For behold, the darkness shall
cover the earth, and gross darkness the people; but
the Lord shall arise upon thee, and His glory
shall be seen upon thee.*

Isaiah 60:1-2

Little Girl Lost

Little girl lost, always wandering alone
In search of a place for her heart to call home
Where is it, you journey; to what destination?
Do you hope to find someone to answer the question?

To whom would you listen; in whom could you trust?
Having learned that protecting yourself, is a must
With walls of defense to separate you
What can anyone say? What can anyone do?

With your feelings all buried too deep for detection
And your heart held prisoner, by fear of rejection
Who has the answer and who holds the key
To unlock this prison and set this child free?

Lost in the darkness that covers her soul
She desperately cries, "God, you're my last hope!"
"If you hear my cry, Lord come to me now!"
"I want to be free; I just don't know how!"

From deep in her spirit, a voice, soft and tender
Saying, "Yes my child, it is time to surrender"
"I see your distress and I hear when you cry"
"I know how you struggle; I know how you try"

"I formed you, my child, from the dust of the earth"
"And I knew my purpose for you, before birth"

"All I have planned, I am ready to do"
"But you see, until now, I've been waiting on you!"

"At last, you are tired, and have cried out to me"
"Now cast all your burdens and cares, at my feet"
"Be filled with my Spirit; endued with my power"
"I'll make you a *'Light to the world'* in this hour!"

"Now lift up your voice with a joyful sound"
"And spread the *Good News* that the lost can be found!"
"Be a soldier for God, as you take up your cross"
"No longer remembered, as Little Girl Lost!"

*For the Son of man is come to seek and to
save that which was lost.*

Luke 19:10

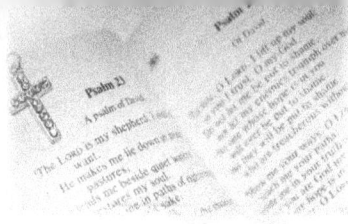

Commitment

My heart is fixed; my mind is stayed
On the Savior, who overcame death and the grave
And descended into the dark corners of hell
To rescue a sinner, like me

Oh God, your wrath would have been my portion
If not for the great sacrifice of you own Son
Now seated in heaven, at your mighty right hand
To make intercession, for me

May all that I am, and all that I do
Accomplish one purpose: to glorify you
I lay down my life, and take up my cross
To follow, wherever you lead

Sherry L Anthamatten © 1998
Poetry, Prayer and Praise Vol. II.

My heart is fixed, O God, my heart is fixed:

Psalms 57:7

Thou wilt keep him in perfect peace,
whose mind is stayed on thee;

Isaiah 26:3

Then said Jesus unto his disciples,
if any man will come after me,
Let him deny himself, and take up his cross,
and follow me.
For whosoever will save his life shall lose it:
And whosoever will lose his life for my sake
shall find it.
For what is a man profited, if he shall gain the whole
world, and lose His own soul?
Or what shall a man give in exchange for his soul?
For the Son of Man shall come in the glory
of His Father
with his angels; and then He shall reward every man
according to his works.

Matthew 16:24-25 & 27

Keep It Simple

If we will keep it simple, God's not hard to understand
He promises His wisdom to all who ask of Him
His Word is like a lamp of light to help us find the way
To overcome the challenges we face, from day to day

If any of you lacks wisdom, he should ask God,
Who gives generously to all without finding fault,
And it will be given to him.

James 1:5

Thy Word is a lamp unto my feet,
And a light unto my path.

Psalms 119:105

For the Lord grants wisdom!
His every Word is a treasure of knowledge and
understanding,
He grants good sense to the godly, His saints.
He is their shield, protecting them and
guarding their pathway.
He shows how to distinguish right from wrong,
How to find the right decision every time.

Proverbs 2:6-9 (The Living Bible)

Lord, Cleanse My Lips

Before you now, Lord, I kneel to pray
Offering up sacrifices of praise
I bless you with all of my heart and my soul;
from my tongue letting heavenly languages roll
Forgiveness and mercy, I ask of you, Lord
For my unruly lips sin against you in word
Let all foolish talk be removed from my mouth
I can't do it alone Lord, I'm asking your help
To cleanse out the poison and quench fires of hell
Letting only the truth of your Word richly dwell
Lord, make of my mouth a pure vessel of gold
From which living rivers of water will flow

Then said I, Woe is me! For I am undone;
Because I am a man of unclean lips.
And I dwell in the midst of a people of unclean lips;
For mine eyes have seen the King, the Lord of hosts.
Then flew one of the Seraphim unto me,
having a live coal in his hand,
Which he had taken with the tongs from of the altar:
And he laid it upon my mouth, and said,
Lo, this hath touched thy lips;
And thine iniquity is taken away, and thy sin purged.

Isaiah 6:5-7

The Master Plan

My Lord, you are a mighty God
All power is held in your hand
What kind of God is this, who cares
For a creature, so lowly, as man

I am only a vessel of earthen flesh
Your ways are far and above
How can I ever, understand
A God of such mercy and love?

Oh, let me see your face, my Lord
I seek you with all of my heart
My eyes may see only dimly, now
But, a new transformation will start

As I take off the "old man", and cast him, aside
I will take on the mind of your Christ
And He will begin to restore and renew
'Til at last, I can see, through His eyes

My Lord, you are a mighty God
All power is held in your hand
Yet now, I see that loving me
Has been your "Master Plan"!

*...if a man love me, he will keep my words:
And my Father will love him, and we will come unto him,
and make our abode with him.
John 14:23*

This New Day

My alarm clock announces a new day to start
I will pause for a moment to open my heart
To let my first thought and my first spoken word
Be, "Good morning, Jesus! I praise you, my Lord!"

I rejoice in you, God, and this day you have made
Forgive all my sin by your mercy and grace
Let your will be done, in and through me, today
As your Spirit leads me, each step of the way

Your joy is my strength and your love is my light
And I walk by faith, in your Word, not by sight
So now, as I rise to meet this new day
I commit it to you, my Lord, have your way

O God, thou art my God; early will I seek Thee.
Psalm 63:1

This is the day which the Lord hath made;
We will rejoice and be glad in it.
Psalm 118:24

Let my mouth be filled with thy praise and with thy
honour all the day.
Psalm 71:8

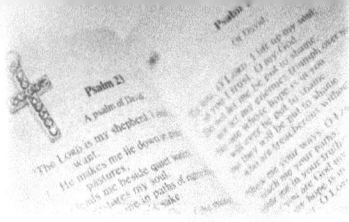

Mercy and Grace

God, you have promised your grace to the humble
Angels to lift up my feet, lest I stumble
Knowing my flesh will be tempted, of sin
You make provision for mercy, again

Conviction and guidance, your Spirit will bring
That my hand might touch not, the unclean thing
Though I must walk through, dark shadows of death
Your Word in my heart, will shed light on my path

If into the pit of destruction, I fall
The voice of my Shepherd, will faithfully call
"Come out, from among them! I am the Way!"
"My sheep know my voice and they will not stray"

By my own name, and you are calling me, tenderly
Out of my trouble, Lord, you will deliver me!

God resisteth the proud,
and giveth grace to the humble.

I. Peter 5:5

...turn unto the Lord your God;
for he is gracious and merciful,
Slow to anger, and of great kindness,

Joel 2:13

Wherefore come out from among them,
and be ye separate, saith the Lord,
And touch not the unclean thing;
and I will receive you.

II. Corinthians 6:17

...and He calleth His own sheep by name,
and leadeth them out.
And when He putteth forth His own sheep,
He goeth before them,
And the sheep follow Him;
for they know His voice.

John 10:3-4

My Lord, My Love

My heart wrenches inside me with yearning and longing
To be in your presence, my Lord and my Love
I know full satisfaction and the joy of belonging
Are awaiting me in the bride's chamber, above
Draw near to me now, Lord of my affection
For you are my breath, and the beat of my heart
Redeemed from the darkness of sin, by your suffering
By love, I am sealed; with blood, I am bought
Still I walk in the flesh, but reborn of your Spirit
An outcast and foreigner now, in this place
How long would you have me to wait and endure it
Until you will grant me to look on your face
The pains of my labor grow stronger, each moment
My approaching deliverance, will soon be revealed
The heavens will flee, at the sound of your trumpet
Then will all desire of my heart be fulfilled

For as a young man marrieth a virgin,
so shall thy sons marry Thee,
and as the bridegroom rejoiceth over the bride,
so shall thy God rejoice over thee.
Isaiah 62:5

Thanksgiving and Praise

This is the day that the Lord has made
I'll be glad and rejoice, with thanksgiving and praise
Oh bless the Lord Jesus, my heart and my soul
Forget not, the mercy and love He has shown
Giver of Life and God of Creation
Precious Redeemer, Lord of salvation
I lift up my voice and lift up my hands
Singing, "Glory and honor to God's Holy Lamb!"
Christ Jesus, my Savior, I love and adore you
And no other gods shall I worship, before you

*Enter into His gates with thanksgiving
and into His courts with praise;
Be thankful unto Him, and bless His holy name.
For the Lord is good; His mercy is everlasting;
and His truth endureth to all generations.*

Psalm 100:4-5

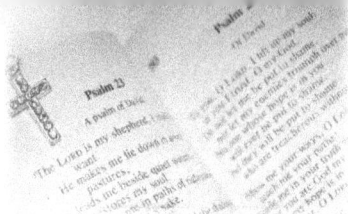

Offering

God, you are my source. Oh hear me, I pray
And give me each tool, as it's needed today
To accomplish my part in your purpose and plan
Take my body, my soul and all that I am
You laid down your life, to pay for my sin
Now, I lay my life down, in your mighty hand
I pray, you accept the offering I bring
To be used to the glory, of Jesus, my King

I beseech you therefore, brethren,
by the mercies of God,
That ye present your bodies a living sacrifice,
Holy, acceptable unto God,
which is your reasonable service.
And be not conformed to this world;
But be ye transformed by the renewing of your mind,
That ye may prove what is that good, and acceptable,
And perfect will of God.

Romans 12:1-2

The Quiet Heart

The quiet heart does willingly wait
Understanding that patience is worked by faith

Tribulation must come, with trial and test
But, the quiet heart finds solace and rest

My God is a refuge and tower of strength
He shelters me safely beneath His wings

The temple of God will not be defiled
That He builds in the quiet heart, of His child

***

Be beautiful inside, in your hearts,
with the lasting charm of a gentle and quiet spirit
which is so precious to God.

I. Peter 3:4
(The Living Bible)

The Handmaiden

There's an angel of mercy among us
Reaching out gentle hands full of love
Speaking words to encourage and comfort
By the promise of Father above

She looks well to the ways of those she adores
Always holding us close to her heart
And if we reach the point where her patience would end
That's the place her long-suffering will start

She shows forth the fruits, of the Spirit of God
So merciful, gentle and kind
If we look to the core for the strength of her soul
It's the love of our Lord, we will find

Her hand is outstretched to the hungry and poor
The forgotten and lonely and lost
She is drawn to their aid by the call on her heart
Never doubting or counting the cost

She follows the footsteps of one gone before
For the path is made straight where He trod
Only looking to Jesus, for all she will need
Walks the humble handmaiden of God

*Many daughters have done virtuously,
but thou excellest them all.
Give her the fruit of her hands;
and let her own works praise her in the gates.
Psalm 31:29&31*

Victory

Oh God, Your own Spirit is living inside of me
My comfort and help, always leading and guiding me
Spirit of Truth, You have opened my eyes
To see, the earth is all filled with your glory

The power of my enemy, falls by your hand
Every knee has to bow at your mighty command
Though giants raise up fierce weapons of war
I know, the God of Salvation is for me

You gave me a spirit of power and love
Made with me, a covenant sealed with your blood
Your word is my sword and faith is my shield
And the angels of God go before me

The battle is finished; the victory won
Satan defeated, by God's holy Son!
Christ Jesus is risen and powers of darkness
Must flee from the light of His glory

But thanks be to God, which giveth us the victory
through our Lord, Jesus Christ.
Therefore, my beloved brethren,
Be steadfast, unmovable,
always abounding in the work of the Lord
Forasmuch as ye know that
your labour is not in vain in the Lord.

I. Corinthians 15:57

...and this is the victory that overcometh the world,
even our faith.

I. John 5:4

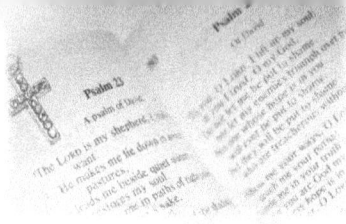

The Vision

In the night a vision was given to me
Something precious that Jesus allowed me to see
A door in the heavenlies, swung open wide
And I was invited to "Come, look inside,"
I stepped up to meet Him, and taking my hand.
He said, "Look, and describe what you see, if you can."

I said, "the place is all filled with glorious light,
And there, in the center, a throne of pure white
And upon that throne there is seated a figure,
Surrounded with clouds, through which, I can see her
I see that she wears a heavily jeweled crown
And intricate tapestries make up her gown."

In my heart, I knew, this must be a queen
I turned to the Lord, asking, "What does this mean?"
And just as I whispered, "I don't understand,"
He said, "Look, and describe what you see, if you can."

So, turning again, and lifting my eyes:
The queen is now, standing; and to my surprise
The most beautiful light shines from her face
I can only describe it, as glorious grace!

Now, walking toward me, her lovely warm smile
Speaks, ever so gently, "Come, visit awhile.
You are welcome here, sister. Don't be afraid.
Come, see all the wonders that Jesus has made!"
I turned to the Lord: and He said, once again
"Look, and describe what you see, if you can."

So I stepped through the cloud: Now, I stand with the queen.
But, there are no words, to describe what I've seen!
Everything that my heart desires or holds dear,
And all that I ever have loved, is right here!
What ear has not heard and eye has not seen,
Is far and above, what my mind can conceive!

Now, standing beside me, I hear Jesus say,
"I've promised that I would prepare you a place!"
Then, setting the heavily jeweled crown, on my head
Whispered, "You are redeemed, by the blood that I shed
I promise to finish, in you, what I start
And you shall reign with me, as Queen of My Heart!"

I pray, through this vision, that came in the night
All my sisters will come, knowing Jesus, as Christ
Look into His eyes, as He offers His hand
Please, look! And describe what you see, if you can!

In my Father's house are many mansions:
If it were not so, I would have told you.
And if I go and prepare a place for you,
I will come again and receive you unto myself;
that where I am, there ye may be also.
John 14:2-3

Eye hath not seen, nor ear heard, neither have
entered into the heart of man, the things which God
hath prepared for them that love Him.
I Corinthians 2:9

And I, John saw the holy city, new Jerusalem,
Coming down from God out of heaven,
prepared as a bride adorned for her husband.
Revelation 21:2

You Reign

High and exalted, far and above
Power and majesty, mercy and love
Come my Lord Jesus, set up your throne
And reign in my heart, King of Kings

Ancient of days, now to eternity
Holy and Sovereign, Glorious Trinity
Come my Lord Jesus, set up your throne
And reign in my heart, King of Kings

The Lord reigns; let the earth rejoice
Psalms 97:1

Wherefore God also hath highly exalted Him,
that at the name of Jesus, every knee should bow
and that every tongue should confess
that Jesus Christ is Lord, to the glory of the Father.
Philippians 2:9-11

But unto the Son, He {God the Father} saith,
"Thy throne, O God, is forever and ever
Hebrews 1:8
(emphasis added)

For He is Lord of lords, and King of kings
Revelation 17:14

Bride's Chamber

From the deepest parts of my spirit
From the depths of my heart and my soul
With groanings that cannot be uttered
Perfect love found in You, You, alone

Silent tears are my only expression
Oh, the joy overflows as I weep
In the chamber of grace, where we kiss the Son's face
It is here that deep calleth to deep

❦

Draw me, we will run after thee;
the King hath brought me into his chambers:
we will be glad and rejoice in thee,
we will remember thy love more than wine;
the upright love thee

Song of Solomon 1:4

Kiss the Son…
Blessed are all they that put their trust in Him

Psalms 2:12

"Joy unspeakable and full of glory!"

I. Peter 1:8

The Christian Life

We are the redeemed, the forgiven, the blessed
For to us our God has given His best
His only Son, Jesus was given, to save
The lost who were bound by death, hell and the grave
We are the redeemed, the forgiven, the blessed
The life of the Christian is God's very best

For God so loved the world,
that He gave His only begotten Son,
That whosoever believeth in Him should not perish,
But have everlasting life.

John 3:16

If God be for us, who can be against us?
He that spared not His own Son,
but delivered Him up for us all,
How shall He not,
with Him also freely give us all things?

Romans 8:31-32

Thanks be to God for His unspeakable gift.
II. Corinthians 9:15

Enduring Faith

Search your heart, daily; purge out unbelief
Your faith is the treasure but doubt is the thief
That comes to destroy and to kill and lay-waste
Herein lies your victory; enduring faith!

The thief cometh not, but for to steal,
and to kill, and to destroy:
I am come that they might have life,
and that they might have it more abundantly.

John 10:10

Be assured and understand that the trial
and proving of your faith
bring out endurance and steadfastness and patience.
But let endurance and steadfastness
and patience have full play
and do a thorough work, so that you may be [people]
perfectly and fully developed
[with no defects] lacking in nothing

James 1:3-4 (The Amplified Bible)

This is the victory that overcometh the world
Even our faith.

I. John 5:4

Enduring The Desert

Oh, desolate wilderness, dry scorching heat
Distorting my vision and burning my feet
Deafening silence resounds in my ear
That searches, the voice of my shepherd, to hear
My heart, it would seem, should be crushed by the weight
But for the upholding, of enduring faith

I would have lost heart.
Unless I had believed that I would see
the goodness of the Lord
in the land of the living

Psalms 27:13

Moreover (let us also be full of joy now!)
Let us exalt and triumph in our troubles
and rejoice in our sufferings,
knowing that pressure and affliction and hardship
produce patient and unswerving endurance.

Romans 5:3
(The Amplified Bible)

Faith And Your Words

Hold tight your profession of faith and be bold
No matter what happens, don't loosen your hold
Don't look to the left or be turned to the right
Remember, It's not flesh and blood that you fight
But spirits of darkness are unleashed in words
Keep a guard on your lips and the victory is yours

❦

*Let us hold fast the profession
of our faith without wavering;*
Hebrews 10:23

*For we wrestle not against flesh and blood
but against principalities, against powers,
against the rulers of darkness of the world.*
Ephesians 6:12

Death and life are in the power of the tongue.
Proverbs 18:21

*Set a guard O Lord, over my mouth.
Keep watch over the door of my lips.*
Psalms 141:3

Fountains Of Mercy

I was bound by a curse of sin
Without a way to be free
But the God of Heaven came down, from His throne
To be made a curse for me

There is one, so full of love,
forgiveness and compassion
Fountains of mercy flowing down,
with the blood of His passion

With His own blood He made me clean but I turned
away from Him
Then from my shame, I called on His name
And Jesus took me back, again

There is one, in need of love; of beauty for the ashes
Fountains of mercy flowing down,
from His heart of compassion

*For we have not an high priest which cannot be touched
with the feeling of our infirmities; but was in all points
tempted like as we are, yet without sin. Let us therefore
come boldly unto the throne of grace, That we may
obtain mercy, and find grace to help in time of need.*
Hebrews 4:15-16

To God Be The Glory

Our Father has a purpose for each of us, to fill
So He distributes gifts to us, according to His will
Only for His greater purpose should our gifts be used
He sends us out, to seek the lost; to take them His
Good News
So let this be our prayer that rises up before His throne
"Lord, keep us faithful always to your will and not our own"

Now in these latter days, we see His Spirit pouring out
But God says, judgment will begin at first, in His own house
So let the prayers of all the saints, as this great judgment starts
Be, "Father, keep us humble in the motives of our hearts"
And let us be reminded as we carry out your plan
That every good and perfect gift is given by your hand"

So Father, let the gifts you've given never be abused
But to the glory of our God, let all our gifts be used

*For of Him and through Him and to Him,
are all things:
to whom be glory for ever. Amen.*

Romans 11:36

Blessed Day

Lord, let this be a blessed day
Each moment, Jesus, have your way
Direct my steps; I will obey
As I walk through this blessed day

Anoint my eyes, anoint my ears
Speak to me Lord; your servant hears
I'll keep my mind and eyes on you
To see the wondrous works, you do

I thank you, that you hear my prayer
Lord, thanks for always being there
I give this day, right from the start
To you, Lord of my life and heart

Sherry L. Anthamatten ©1998
Poetry Prayer and Praise Vol. II.

*This is the day which the Lord hath made;
we will rejoice and be glad in it.*

Psalms 118:24

God's Desire

You tell me that you need me
But how could this be true
What could I have to give
But that, which I have drawn from you
What could the heart of God desire
For what could your heart yearn
But that the love, you've given me
Be willingly returned

***

Jesus said unto him,
Thou shall love the, Lord, thy God with all by heart,
and with all thy soul, and with all thy mind.
This is the first and great commandment.

Matthew 22:37-38

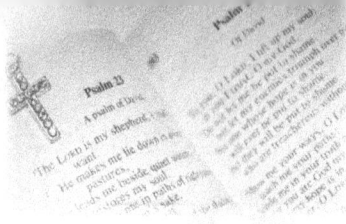

Arise Shine

Arise, shine! Oh arise, shine
Arise, for your light has come
And the glory of the Lord is risen upon thee
So, arise and shine His light for all to see

Arise, shine! Oh arise, shine
Arise for your light has come
Jesus is the light of salvation to the lost
So, arise, you soldiers of the cross

Arise, shine! Oh arise, shine
Arise for your light has come
I heard Him call my name
And He said, "Now, is the time
For the Church of Jesus Christ
To rise and shine!"

Arise, shine! Oh arise, shine
Arise for your light has come
A city set upon a hill; a light unto all men
Will arise and shine the light to lead them in

Arise, shine!

Arise shine; for thy light is come,
and the glory of the Lord is risen upon thee.
For behold, the darkness shall cover the earth,
and gross darkness the people;
but the Lord shall arise upon thee,
and His glory shall be seen upon thee.

Isaiah 60:1-2

The Hands Of Jesus

I have seen the hands of Jesus, masculine and strong
Reach out to turn and redirect a life that has gone wrong
And I have seen the hands of Jesus, delicate and meek
Reach out to bind the soldier's wounds and bathe their
weary feet

Sometimes the hands are young and smooth and
sometimes drawn with age
That reach out to the broken hearts to wipe their tears away
His hands, upon the shoulders of the widows, growing old
Speak messages to reassure: "I'm here;, you're not alone"

Sometimes His hands are lily white and sometimes ebony
Because the hands of Jesus now, reach out through you and me
His hands will feed the hungry soul and give the dry, to drink
And reach out to the downcast one to offer hope and
strength

And as we lift our hands to Him, our Lord will never fail
To fill our hands with power, to withhold the gates of hell
So, let us lift up holy hands in worship and in prayer
Knowing, as we do, the hands of Jesus will be there

And whatsoever ye do in word or deed,
do all in the name of the Lord Jesus,
Giving thanks to God and the Father by Him.

Colossians 3:17

Here I Am

I have measured out the heavens with my fingers
Poured the oceans, from the hollow of my hand
But, I love you, best of all, of my creation
When you call on me, I'll answer, "Here I Am"

Who hath measured the waters in the hollow of His
hand, and meted out the heaven with the span

Isaiah 40:12

We love Him, because He first loved us.

I. John 4:19

Then shalt thou call, and the Lord shall answer;
thou shat cry, and He shall say, "Here I am".

Isaiah 58:9

The Garden Of The Lord

How lovely the first flush of bloom
The bringing forth of life
And how we grieve to see those flowers fade

But in the garden of Our Lord
We have this blessed hope
That Jesus has prepared for us, a place

Unless a seed fall to the ground
It shall abide alone
But if it fall, again new life is made

How glorious that flush of bloom
That brings eternal life
And in His garden, flowers never fade

The grass withereth, the flower fadeth,
but the word of our God shall stand forever.

Isaiah 40:8

Verily, verily I say unto you,
Except a corn of wheat fall
Into the ground and die, it abideth alone:
but if it die, it bringeth forth much fruit.

John 12:24

Their soul shall be as a watered garden;
and they shall not sorrow any more at all.

Jeremiah 31:12

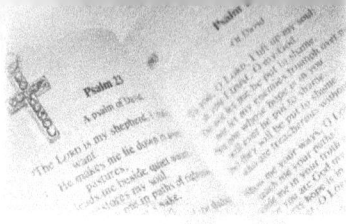

Not Guilty

In Jesus, I'm washed and made white, as the snow
Though before, I was wretched and filthy
My sins could outnumber the sands of the seas
But the Lord has declared me, "Not guilty"

I once was addicted and sick with disease
But now, I am healed and set free
All the burden's removed and the yoke is destroyed
By the presence of Jesus in me

In a crowd I was lonely; inside, so afraid
And my own fear of death would have killed me
Had my Savior not died, so that I might have life
Through His blood that declared me, "Not guilty"

Having chosen us, He called us to come to Him;
And when we came, He declared us "Not guilty"
Filled us with Christ's goodness,
gave us right standing with Himself,
And promised us His glory.

Romans 8:30
(The Living Bible)

Precious Moments

How precious are these moments, Lord
I spend alone with you
With nothing to distract or interfere
How wonderful this secret place
I've found beneath your wings
And knowing I will always find you here

He that dwelleth in the secret place of the Most High
Shall abide under the shadow of the Almighty.
I will say of the Lord, He is my refuge and my fortress:
My God; in Him will I trust.

Psalm 91:1-2

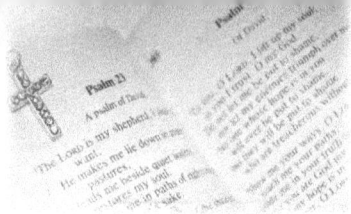

The Hideaway

Come away my beloved! Run to the hideaway!
I will provide a safe place of refuge
Come away my beloved! Run to the hideaway!
I want to be a strong tower for you

Here in the hideaway, no harm shall come to you
Now shall I gather you into my nest
I am your hideaway! My wings shall cover you
Come my beloved and I'll give you rest

Drink of my fountains of peace that restore to you
All that was stolen and lost through the years
Share my communion; pour out your heart to me
Let the sweet sound of your song fill my ears

Come let my chambers of love be your hiding place
God's holy covenant joins you to me
Come away, my beloved! Come know the mystery
Blessed, this day of our union, shall be!

My beloved spake and said unto me
"Rise up, my love, my fair one, and come away!"

Song of Solomon 2:10

Thou art my hiding place;

Psalms 32:7

He shall cover you with His feathers.
And under His wings you shall take refuge.

Psalms 91:4

Come unto me, all ye that labour and are heavy laden
And I will give you rest.

Matthew 11:28

My Only God

My God, you are my only God
I'll have no gods, before you
In striving never to offend
Let all I do be for you

Distractions, I now put away
That seek to capture me
And set my heart on things above
That please and honor thee

Oh God, you are my only God
I'll have no gods before you
With all my body, heart and soul
I worship and adore you

Thou shalt have no other Gods before me.

Exodus 20:3

Set your affection on things above,
not things on this earth.

Colossians 3:2

Thou shalt love the Lord thy God with all thy heart,
and with all thy soul, and with all thy mind.

Matthew 22:37

I beseech you therefore, brethren,
by the mercies of God
That ye present your bodies a living sacrifice, holy,
acceptable unto God, which is your reasonable service.

Romans 12:1

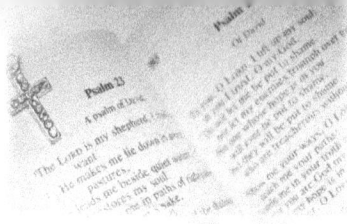

Pray for the Peace of Jerusalem

Pray for the peace, of Jerusalem
Holy City of God
Come Prince of Peace, to Jerusalem
And reign, our King, from your throne

We are the children of Abraham
Blessed by the promises made to him
Heirs to God's holy covenant
Sealed by the blood, of His Lamb

Pray for the peace of Jerusalem
Holy City, of God
Come Prince of Peace, to Jerusalem
And reign, our King, from your throne

Pray for the peace of Jerusalem:
They shall prosper that love thee

Psalm 122:6

And I will bless them that bless thee,
and curse him that curseth thee:

Genesis 12:3

And if ye be Christ's, then are ye Abraham's seed,
and heirs according to the promise.

Galatians 3:29

Thy throne, O God is for ever and ever

Psalm45:6

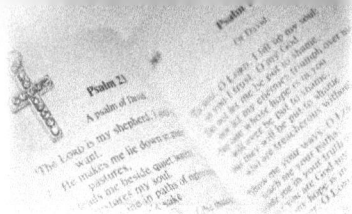

Precious Jesus

Oh you are sweet, so sweet, my Lord
My precious, loving Savior
How tender are your mercies, Lord
How blessed is your favor

This earthen jar cannot contain
The wealth of love I know
You fill me up and when I'm full
This love must overflow

So let the world call me a fool
If I'm a fool for you
To give my life would be the very least
That I could do

No greater love has any man
Than this you freely gave
Oh Holy One, that you would die
My wretched life, to save

If I could search a million years
Your love would be the sweetest
So I will never cease to worship you
My Precious Jesus!

Greater love hath no man than this,
That a man lay down his life for his friends.

John 15:13

I will bless the Lord at all times: His praise will
continually be in my mouth

Psalm 34:1

The Promised Place

I know your suffering, Children
Please know that I am here
And though you weep in secret
I'll wipe away your tears
And when you whisper, "Help me"
The one who loves you hears
I have bought you with my blood and you are mine
I was, in all ways, tempted
As you're tempted on the earth
The greatest suffering that a man can face
I gladly bore the cross to take the curse of all your sin
So I could bring you to the Promised Place

I go to prepare a place for you.
And if I go and prepare a place for you,
I will come again and receive you unto myself;
that where I am, there ye may be also.

John 14:2-3

I reckon that the sufferings of this present time
are not worthy to be compared
with the glory which shall be revealed in us.

Romans 8:18

The Robe

I only ask, please understand this thing I tell you
For so often I have been misunderstood
I stand before you born again and bound for glory
Just because the Lord my God, He is so good

Do you see this robe of righteousness I'm wearing
Though my sins were scarlet now they're white as snow
You see it's only by the cleansing blood of Jesus
My filthy rags could have been changed into this robe

I was dying, 'til He gave His Life to save me
I was blind, 'til He became my Light to see
I was naked, 'til He wrapped His robe around me
Now all my shame is covered, by His love for me

Come now, and let us reason together, saith the Lord:
Though your sins be as scarlet, they shall be white as snow;

Isaiah 1:18

I will greatly rejoice in the Lord,
my soul shall be joyful in my God;
For He hath clothed me with the garments of salvation,
He hath covered me with the robe of righteousness

Isaiah 61:10

Thy Will Be Done

Dear God, there are so many needs
And Lord, you know them all
How could I even name them one by one
I don't know all the answers; only you can see the heart
And so I pray, "Dear God, Thy will be done"

Your will is always perfect
And your ways are just and true
Lord, there is none in earth or heaven
To compare with you
Oh God, there are so many needs
But you will meet each one
I simply pray, "Dear God, Thy will be done"

*...your heavenly Father knoweth that you
have need of all these things.
But seek ye first the kingdom of God,
and His righteousness;
and all these things shall be added unto you.*

Matthew 6:32-33

*...God shall supply all your need
according to His riches in glory by Christ Jesus.*

Philippians 4:19

Today

Today again, my Savior is standing at the gate
How long this world's distractions have caused my
Lord to wait
Though many times I've heard Him call, today He calls again
That I might turn and take one step toward His
outstretched hand

Today that I might listen and turn to heed His voice
Let go the world's distractions for one eternal choice
Today, that I might lift my eyes to Him, perhaps to see
That all I have been searching for, is waiting there, for me

*For He is our God; and we are the people of His
pasture, and the sheep of His hand
To day if ye will hear His voice,
harden not your heart*

Psalm 95:7

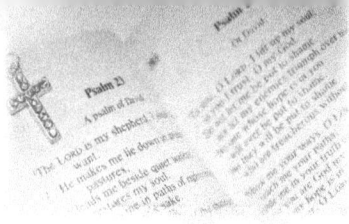

Savior

When I mourn, you turn my grief into a dance
When all hope is gone, you give a second chance
When my sinful nature lures me to it's trap
Again I find you standing in the gap

And if I'm frightened or I'm feeling lonely
Your strong, right arm is always there to hold me
When friends forsake, accuse and won't believe me
I'll stand because I know you'll never leave me

Jesus, Lord and Savior, you have saved me from my sin
And every day you prove to be my Savior once again
A Savior, who will rescue me each time I call your name
A Savior, who is there to heal my hurts and ease my pain

The Savior, who had love enough, my empty heart to fill
Forgave my sin and saved my soul, and is my Savior, still

Fear not, for I am with you;
be not dismayed, for I am your God.
I will strengthen you, I will uphold you
With My righteous right hand.

Isaiah 41:10
(New King James)

Lo, I am with you alway, even to the end of the world.
Amen.

Matthew 28:20

Sweet Communion

Come follow me now, to commune with the Savior
No place will you find quite as sweet
As the table prepared for communion with Him
Where we gather to sit at His feet

In His presence is found every answer we seek
And provision for all of our needs
Come follow me now, to commune with the Savior
No place will you find quite as sweet

As we drink of the cup and remember His suffering
The precious blood covers our sin
And the bread as His body, is broken for us
For the healing found only in Him

If we open our hearts in response to His knocking
He promises He will come in
And will dine with the children, who come to His table
To share sweet communion with Him

And He took bread, and gave thanks,
and brake it, and gave unto them saying,
This is my body which is given for you:
this do in remembrance of me.
Likewise the cup after supper, saying,
This is the new testament in my blood,
which is shed for you.

Luke 22:20

Behold, I stand at the door and knock:
If any man hear My voice, and open the door,
I will come in and dine with him, and he with Me.

Revelation 3:20
(New King James)

Treasure Search

With every new dawn tender mercies renewed
And manna from Heaven each day is our food
A cloud and a pillar of fire in the night
God's hand is upon us to faithfully guide
Living water is poured out in streams through the desert
Whosoever will search shall discover His treasure

The Kingdom of Heaven is like a treasure
a man discovered in a field.. In his excitement,
he sold everything he owned to get enough money
to buy the field, and get the treasure, too!

Matthew 13:44 (The Living Bible)

Do not lay up for yourselves treasures on earth,
where moth and rust destroys and
where thieves break in and steal;
but lay up for yourselves treasures in heaven,
where moth nor rust destroys and
where thieves do not break in and steal.
For where your treasure is,
there your heart will be also.

Matthew 6:19-21

Unity

Let us know our gift of grace
And see it shine on every face
Of every child, of every race
And bring us back together

❦

Christ gave each one of us the special gift of grace.

Ephesians 4:7
(New Century Version)

We are no longer Jews or Greeks
or slaves or free men
or even merely men or women,
but we are all the same;
we are Christians; we are one in Christ Jesus

Galatians 3:28
(The Living Bible)

By this shall all men know that ye are my disciples
If ye have love one to another

John 13:35

Everything I Do

I'm going to lay down all my sins and praise the Lord
I'm going to lift up holy hands and praise the Lord
I'm going to stand up on my feet and praise the Lord
Then I will get down on my knees and praise the Lord

Let everything I do glorify Him
Let all I do be done unto the Lord
Let the words of my mouth and meditations of my heart
Be pleasing in your sight, oh God

*Whatsoever ye do in word or deed,
do all in the name of the Lord Jesus,
giving thanks to God and the Father by Him.*

Colossians 3:17

*For of Him, and through Him, and to Him, are all things;
to whom be glory for ever. Amen*

Romans 11:36

*Let the words of my mouth,
and the meditation of my heart,
be acceptable in thy sight, O Lord*

Psalms 19:14

Can You See Me

What do you see, looking at me
My imperfection, my inability
Do I provoke your sympathy
Is that all you can see in me

I'd like to show you, if I might
How I appear in Jesus sight
A sinner saved, a wrong made right
A miracle, a shining light

Can you see me through Jesus' eyes

… For the Lord. seeth not as man seeeth;
for man looketh on the outward appearance,
but the Lord looketh on the heart.

I. Samuel 16:7

The Vessel

The Lord says, It is not a perfect people that I seek
But one, whose hearts are humbled, and yielded up, to me
The clay that I find pliable, to the workings of my hand
Will I reshape and mold, as only I, the Potter, can

To make of clay, a vessel, that is fit to serve the King
Cannot be done by your own works, or any human means
The vessel must be emptied, of pride and selfish will
So, by God's Holy Spirit, the vessel can be filled

For clay to turn to gold, it must be cleansed and purified
With all-consuming fire, in which the vessel must be tried
And when my people, by their faith, have stood the fiery test
With praise, and with rejoicing, they will come into my rest

Then, the King shall look on these, as vessels of great worth
And send them out, to take His glory, into all the earth
Blessed is the workmanship, the Potter's hand has wrought
To pour out living water, flowing from the heart of God

Behold, as the clay is in the potter's hand
So are ye in My hand.

Jeremiah 18:6

But in a great house there are
not only vessels of gold and of silver,
but also of wood and of earth;
and some to honor, and some to dishonor.
If a man therefore purge himself from these,
he shall be a vessel unto honor, sanctified,
and meet for the Masters use,
and prepared unto every good work.

II.Timothy 2: 20–21

My Front Porch

Well Lord, we've had some good, long talks, out on this
old front porch
I love to sit here, spending time with you
And in the evening, when it's cool, and neighbors come
outside
They like to sit a spell, and visit, too

Seems like I've sat here, on this porch, and watched the
whole world change
Old things torn down, replaced with something new
And somewhere, I lost count of all the friends and dear,
old folks
That since, have gone on home, to be with You

Well Lord, it kinda' gets me thinkin', 'bout those
"streets of gold"
And all those wonders "eye hath never seen"
I'd like to think, there'll be a mansion, with a big front porch
And friends and loved ones, waiting there, for me

I'm sure, it will be wonderful, whatever You've prepared
And one day, I'll leave this old place behind me
But 'til the day the angels come, to carry me on home
Well Lord, You'll always know, where You can find me

Godliness with contentment is great gain.
For we brought nothing into this world,
And it is certain we can carry nothing out.

I. Timothy 6:6-7

In my Father's house are many mansions;
if it were not so, I would have told you.
I go to prepare a place for you.
And if I go and prepare a place for you,
I will come again,
And receive you unto myself; that where I am,
There ye may be also.

John 14:2-3

Like You

I glorify you, Lord; you are my, one desire
Come live inside my heart, and let Your Spirit's fire
Do all Your work in me, to make me be like You

I want to be like you; I want to see through your eyes
I want to feel with your heart; Lord, Help me to realize
What needs to change in me, so that I can be like you

My God, I am created in your image
Now, let your perfect will be done in me
In my thoughts and in my words, and everything I do
I am predestined to be made, to be like you

I want to be like you; fill me with truth and light
Give me your heart of love, and the mind of Christ
Lord, have your way in me, so, I can be like you .

Therefore be imitators of God,
as well beloved children imitate their Father

Ephesians 5:1
(The Amplified Bible)

For those God foreknew He also
predestined to be conformed
To the likeness of His Son.

Romans 8:9
(New International Version)

Beloved, now are we the sons of God,
and it doth not yet appear what we shall be:
but we know that, when He shall appear,
we shall be like Him;
or we shall see Him as He is.
I. John 3:2

The Waltz

In a dream, I was caught up to Heaven
Face to face with my Savior, my Lord
And I fell to my knees, just to kiss His precious feet
But I scarcely could utter a word

When at last I dared to lift my eyes
I could see His loving hand reaching down
To lift me to my feet, and as He began to speak
Oh His voice, that familiar sweet sound!

Asking, "What would you have me do for you?"
As His arms drew me in, and held me near
Overwhelmed with the joy of His presence
This one request, I softly whispered in His ear

"I just ask, would you waltz with me Jesus
As we glide would you whirl me around
For so long, I have dreamed of the wedding day waltz
At the glorious marriage feast of the Lamb!"

So I ask, "Would you waltz with me, Jesus
As we glide, would you whirl me around
For so long now, I've dreamed of this, wedding day waltz
And the glorious, marriage feast of the Lamb!"

And he saith unto me, "Write
Blessed are they which are called
unto the marriage supper of the Lamb."
And he saith unto me,
"These are the true sayings of God."

Revelation 19:9

A Word of Love

If you have a word of love to say
Don't keep it to yourself
What good are precious gifts of love
If you leave them on the shelf
Waiting for the right occasion
Waiting for some special day
When someone needs, so desperately
A word of love, today

*The Lord God hath given me the tongue of the learned,
that I should know how to speak a word in season
to him that is weary:*

Isaiah 50:4

*Don't just pretend that you love others: really love them.
Hate what is wrong. Stand on the side of good.
Love each other with brotherly affection
and take delight in honoring each other.
Never be lazy in your work,
but serve the Lord enthusiastically.*

Romans 12:9–10 (The Living Bible)

Amazing Love

Oh God, your love amazes me
How can I comprehend
That you would be so merciful
To pay my debt of sin

A debt that I could never pay
One, you could never owe
But yet, you came and left behind
The glory of your throne

Oh yes, your love amazes me
How can I understand
A God of such compassion for
The sinful state of man

For God so loved the world,
that He gave His only begotten Son,
that whosoever believeth in Him should not perish,
but have everlasting life.

John 3:16

What are mortals that you should think of us,
Mere humans that you should care for us?

Psalms 8:4

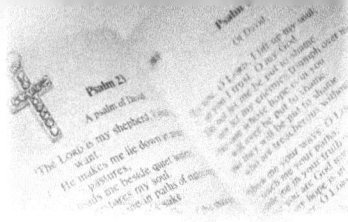

No Regrets

Never leave love unexpressed
No deed undone, no word unsaid
Live every day, as if the last
Then rest in peace with no regrets

Let your light so shine before men,
that they may see your good works,
and glorify your Father which is in heaven.

Matthew 5:17

And whatsoever ye do in word or deed,
do all in the name of the Lord Jesus,
giving thanks to God the Father by Him.

Colossians 3:17

To Know You

Dear Jesus, show me who you are. Please, help me find
the way
Of seeking, with a humble heart, to know you more,
each day
To know you , as Almighty God, in reverential fear
To know you, as the God of Love, a Father's love, so dear
To know you, as the Prince of Peace, my shelter, from
the storm
To know you , as the Savior ,whose great mercy bids
me, "Come"
To know you, as Creator, who breathes life, into dust
To know you, as Immanuel, the mighty "God with us"
To know you more today, my Lord, than I knew, yesterday
I seek you, with a humble heart. Please, help me find
my way

*I count all things but loss for the excellency of the
knowledge of Christ Jesus, my Lord.*

Philippians 3:8

I Just Sing for My Jesus

A piano softly played, as the people began to praise
All God's children gathered there, of one accord
And His presence was so sweet, as we all stood to our feet
Lifting up one voice of worship to our Lord

There was a man with silver hair, I hadn't noticed
standing there
'Til he crossed the room and stepped up to the stage
As the piano softly played, he sang about amazing grace
Unashamed of loving tears that streaked his face

He said, "I just sing for my Jesus, who bore the cross for me
Unashamed of blood and tears that streaked His face
Who still bears the nail-scars on His hands of love that
lifted me
From death to life, by His amazing grace"

As he lifted up his eyes and his hands up to the skies
I thought that it was very plain to see
That it is more than just a song, to a life that has gone wrong
It's amazing grace that saved a wretch like me

He said, "I just sing for my Jesus, who bore the cross for me
Unashamed of blood and tears that streaked His face

Who still bears the nail-scars on His hands of love that lifted me
From death to life, by His amazing grace"

I pray that all who hear will see, and come to know as personally
The Lamb of God, who died for you and me
And although many men are called, I think no other stands so tall
As that dear silver-haired brother, on his knees

*But, He giveeth more grace. Wherefore. He saith,
God. resisteth the the proud,
but giveth grace unto the humble.*

James 4:6

*Let the word of Christ dwell in you richly in all wisdom;
teaching and admonishing one another in psalms
and hymns and spiritual songs,
singing with grace in your hearts to the Lord.*

Colossians 3:16

Lift Up Your Eyes

I can feel a mighty shaking of the ground, beneath my feet
As persecution comes against the Word of Truth, I speak
Though I be hated for His sake, reviled and criticized
God's Word will never pass away; I will not compromise

Everything that can be shaken, will be shaken in this day
But I have a sure foundation, this profession of my faith
When these things begin to happen; all that has been
prophesied
Drawing near is my redemption; Jesus said "Lift up your
eyes!"

Mountains crumble all around me, all the earth is
sinking sand
But the Rock of Truth I stand on, shall endure unto the end
Weapons will be formed against me, in the fire I must
be tried
But I know from where my help comes; Jesus, I lift up
my eyes!

I will keep on looking to you, Source and Object of my Faith
For in perfect peace you keep me, as on you my mind
is stayed
I will run the race before me, for the glory of the prize
As the witnesses in heaven, call to me, "Lift up your eyes!"

In the furnace of affliction, hated and betrayed by all
Many, Lord, will be offended; keep me humble lest I fall
Until the doors of heaven open, to receive the Bride of
Christ
May my lamp be filled and burning, when You call, "Lift
up your eyes!"

When the saints shall bow in worship, there before
God's Holy Lamb
And the books of His remembrance, then are opened in
His hand
I pray that as I bow before Him, at the Judgment Seat of
Christ
I will not be made ashamed, when Jesus says, "Lift up
your eyes!

*I will lift up mine eyes unto the hills,
from whence cometh my help.
My help cometh from the Lord,
which made heaven and earth.*

Psalm 121:1–2

*Unto thee I lift up mine eyes,
O thou that dwellest in the heavens.*

Psalm 123:1

*"And now, little children, abide in Him:
That when He shall appear, we may have confidence
And not be ashamed before Him, at His coming."*

I. John 2:28

A New Name

A new name is written upon a white stone
A name by which I will forever be known
A name God has chosen especially for me
And only He knows what that new name will be

※

*He that hath an ear, let him hear what the Spirit says
unto the churches; To him that overcometh will I give
to eat of the hidden manna, And will give him a white
stone, and in the stone a new name written,
which no man knoweth saving he that receiveth it.*

Revelation 2:17

*Him that overcometh, will I make a pillar in the temple
of my God, and he shall go no more out: and I will write
upon him the name of my God, and the name of the city
of my God, which is new Jerusalem, which cometh down
out of heaven from my God: and I will write upon him
my new name.*

Revelation 4:12

*And the Gentiles shall see thy righteousness, and all
kings thy glory: and thou shall be called by a new
name, which the mouth of the Lord shall name.*

Isaiah 62:2

Paradise Found

There is a paradise ready and waiting
Somewhere in heaven, a place is prepared
Oh how my soul longs to see that sweet paradise
And for the day, I will meet Jesus there

Here in this world, I endure tribulations
Face persecutions and sufferings untold
Yet even now, I have found I have paradise
Peace that runs deep and lies still in my soul

***

*Thou will keep him in perfect peace,
whose mind is stayed on Thee*

Isaiah 26:3

*And the peace of God, which passeth all
understanding, shall keep your hearts and minds
through Christ Jesus*

Philippians 4:7

*Peace I leave with you, my peace I give unto you:
not as the world giveth, give I unto you.
Let not your heart be troubled,
neither let it be afraid.*

John 14:27

Only Jesus

Who can I find to heal my broken heart
Is there anyone there that can mend
Who can I find who will never forsake me
But stay by my side 'til the end

Who can break the grip, of fear when I'm dying
Will anyone walk with me then
Will anyone listen to my pleading heart
And have mercy and love to forgive

Only Jesus can heal a broken heart
Only He who created can mend
Only Jesus will never forsake you
But stay by your side 'til the end
Only Jesus from death has redeemed you
Forever together, to live
Only Jesus can hear your pleading heart
And have mercy and love to forgive

He healeth the broken in heart,
and bindeth up their wounds.

Psalm 147:3

… For, he hath said, "I will never leave thee,
nor forsake thee".

Hebrew 13:5

Yea, though I walk through the valley of the shadow of
death, I will fear no evil: for thou art with me;

Psalm 23:4

For this God is our God, for ever and ever:,
He will be our guide even unto death.

Psalm 48:14

Seed-Time and Harvest

Remember, every word you speak
and every deed you do
Is planted as the seed to bring
a harvest back to you
A seed will always reproduce
after its own kind
So choose the seeds you plant, with care
and keep this thought in mind
The seeds you sow today will bring
results into your life
Be sure to plant the crop you want
to reap, at harvest-time

*Be not deceived, deluded and misled
God will not allow Himself to be mocked
For what ever a man sows
That and that only, is what he will reap*

Galatians 6:7 (Amplified Bible)

*And what ever you do no matter what it is in word or deed
Do everything in the name of the Lord Jesus*

Colossians 3:17 (Amplified Bible)

Who Are You, Lord

Who are you Lord, oh Glorious King
Wonderful Counselor, my Prince of Peace
God of Salvation, Faithful and True
My hearts desire is to know more of you
Holy Blood Sacrifice, given to save
Lamb, who was slain and then rose from the grave
Son of the living God, Jesus the Christ
Show me your mercy and open my eyes
Pillar of Fire, directing my way
You are the sweet Bread of Life, every day
Manna from Heaven, each day I need more
Show me again today, who are you, Lord

Who is this King of glory?
The Lord strong and mighty, The Lord mighty in battle.
Lift up your heads, O ye gates; even lift them up, Ye
everlasting doors;
And the King of glory shall come in.
Who is this King of glory?
The Lord of hosts, He is the King of glory. Selah.

*I count all things but loss
for the excellency of the knowledge
of Christ Jesus, my Lord*

Philippians 3:8

A Silent Prayer

Sometimes I may not really know, what's going on
inside you
But since I know that Jesus does, I know He'll lead and
guide you
So as you listen to His heart, please listen to mine, too
A prayer is being whispered there, from me, to God, for you

But thou, when thou prayest, enter into thy closet,
and when thou hast shut the door,
pray to thy Father which is in secret;
and thy Father which seeth in secret
shall reward thee openly.
for your Father knoweth what things ye
have need of before ye ask Him.

Matthew 6:6&8

True Life

Oh what a blessed and wonderful day
What a glorious day it will be
When I meet with my loved ones who've gone on before
And my Savior, who died for me
Oh what a blessed and wonderful day
When my work here, at last is all done
And I step across time, into eternal life
To find true life has only begun

Those who love their lives will lose them;
but those who hate [have no concern or reguard for]
their lives in this world, will keep true life forever

John 12:25
(New Century & Amplified Bible)

Purpose

Let your smile be quick to all that you meet
Let your presence be tender and loving and sweet
Let the love of the Lord shine brightly through you
That others might see it and know His love too

Be "instant in season and out" as you go
Be ready to witness the source of your hope
Speak often of God and the Savior, who came
Not to judge and can condemn, but to rescue and save

It's the goodness of God that will draw people
And then, with a prayer you can lead them to Him
To be "salt and light", always ready to give
Is our purpose and passion and reason to live

A new commandment I give unto you,
That ye love one another: as I have loved you
That ye also love one another.

John 13:34

Let your light so shine before men,
that they may see your good works,
And glorify your Father which is in heaven.

Matthew 5:16

And we know that all things work together for good
to them that love God, to them who are the called
according to his purpose.

Romans 8:28

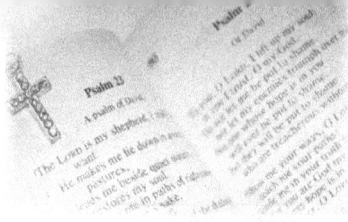

The Fragile Heart

My Precious friend with the fragile heart
Like a vulnerable child, so easily hurt
Run quickly to Father whose strong, loving arms
Reach out to receive you and keep you from harm

And please listen closely to all He will say
His commandments are easy, not hard to obey
For He will enable and order your steps
That lead to new heights and uncover new depths

Of a far greater love than you've known before
It is not of this world, but the Love of the Lord
His yoke is not heavy, intending to break you
His arm will uphold and His love won't forsake you

And though life will challenge you, He'll help you stand
And no one can pluck His child out of His hand

Come unto me, all ye that labor and are heavy laden,
and I will give you rest.
Take my yoke upon you, and learn of me;
for I am meek and lowly in heart:
and ye shall find rest unto your souls.
For my yoke is easy and my burden is light.

Matthew 11:28

My sheep hear my voice, and I know them,
and they follow me:, and I give unto them eternal life;
and they shall never perish, neither shall any man
pluck them out of my hand

John, 10:27–28

Faithful Love

My Faithful Love, draw near to me and spend some time
To let me know you long to be here, by my side
For the love we share is always on my mind
Draw near to me, my Faithful Love, my chosen Bride

Oh yes, I hear you calling me, my Faithful Love
Your voice is sweeter, than the singing of the dove
Just one life with you could never be enough
It has to be eternity, my Faithful Love

Now, the bride and groom long for the wedding day
And the union of the two, shall be displayed
As the city is descending from above
To join the Bride and Christ, her King, in faithful love

Draw near to God and, he will draw near to you.

James, 4:8

*How precious it is Lord, to realize that you
are thinking about the constantly!*

Psalms 139:17,
(The Living Bible)

I will betroth you to Me forever.

Hosea 2:19

*Then I John, saw the holy city, New Jerusalem,
coming down out of heaven from God,
prepared as a bride adorned for her husband.
And I heard a loud voice, saying,
'Behold, the tabernacle of God is with men,
And He will dwell with them,
and they shall be His people.
God Himself will be with them and be their God.*

Revelation 21:2–3

All Is Well

There is a place, where I can go
To be with Jesus, all alone
It is a secret place, where I can dwell
And there, my Savior speaks to me
Sometimes, revealing mysteries
And at times, He only whispers, "All is well"

He leads me by a narrow way
Where there are trials that I must face
And sometimes, I know, I stumble and I fail
That's when I run to my secret place
I close the door, and as I pray
I can hear His sweet voice whisper, "All is well"

"All is well because your name is carved
In the palms of my own hands
Because I knew, my plan for you
Long before the world began
I have called you out of the dark, of night
Now, you're standing in my marvelous light
And as long as you believe me, all is well"

He leads me high, upon the mount
And there, I stand on holy ground
Then sometimes, I walk the valley's lonely trail
But there is one thing that I know
Where Jesus leads me, I will go
And as long, as I have Jesus, all is well

All is well because my name is carved
In the palms of His own hands
Because He knew, His plan for me
Long before the world began
He has called me out of the dark, of night
Now, I'm standing in His marvelous light
And as long as I have Jesus, all is well

He that dwells in the secret place of the most High
shall abide under the shadow of the Almighty
I will say of the Lord, "He is my refuge and my
fortress: My God; in Him will I trust."

Psalms 91:1–2

For I know the plans I have for you, declares the Lord,
plans to prosper you and not to harm you,
plans to give you hope and a future.

Jeremiah 29:11 (NIV)

… that ye should show forth the praises of Him
who hath called you out of darkness
into His marvelous light.

I. Peter 2:9

Behold, I have graven thee upon
the palms of my hands;

Isaiah 49:16

About the Author

Sherry Weese-Anthamatten loved growing up in her small hometown of Drumright, Oklahoma. Her hobbies were ballet, tap and contemporary dance, as well as high school cheerleading. She married her husband Ernest in 1995 and became step-mom to a son and two daughters and has been blessed with three grandchildren.

Sherry's husband Ernest has been involved in ministry outreach since age 21, co-founding Jesus Way Ministries in the 1970's. In 2003, the couple founded Holy Joe's Gathering Place Ministries, Inc. in Broken Arrow; a casual coffee-house type atmosphere with Bible teaching, live Christian bands, including The Holy Joe's House Band led by Ernest who was lead vocalist plus playing keyboard and rhythm guitar. They served Christians of all denominations, as well as providing bus transportation for many people experiencing homelessness and drug and alcohol addictions. The ministry experienced far-reaching effects of salvations and lives changed, with many of the converted becoming volunteer staff for the ministry.

Nursing home ministry has also been a passion for Sherry, where she visits with residents, offering companionship, love and encouragement through her poetry, prayer and God-inspired messages.

Recently, Sherry and Ernest have been able to semi-retire, focusing on publishing Sherry's poetry and other Christian books, and recording songs they have both written and used in ministry over the years. At home, Sherry loves flower gardening, and both she and her husband enjoy doing restoration projects on their 1920 historical home.

They are also devoted "pet parents" to their Shih Tzu, Sissy, and Jack Russell terrier, Jackie.

Asked to describe how she feels about writing, Sherry would say, "I don't write. Writing would be the last thing that I would have chosen. The Lord inspired this poetry. It's more like taking dictation or speaking a "word" of prophecy; I can't make myself do it, as I will. It comes from God, as He wills."

www.ingramcontent.com/pod-product-compliance
Lightning Source LLC
Chambersburg PA
CBHW051829040426
42447CB00006B/432